M000194308

Advance Praise for Delegate Your Book

I've been ghostwriting business books (along with other types) for over thirty years, so it's refreshing to find such a pithy, plain-spoken volume that speaks to the fundamentals of what it takes to create a solid marketing-tool title. Delegate Your Book *by nonfiction ghostwriter Chrissy Das speaks directly to the aspiring author in all businesspeople, smoothly blending jargon with common, almost conversational vernacular. I definitely recommend it for those who understand the value of being an author—and the benefits of teamwork.*

Claudia Suzane
Professional Ghostwriter and Ghostwriting Instructor,
Ghostwriting Professional Designation Program (GPDP)

Can you tell your story or can someone else tell it better? I am all for delegating because it's absolutely necessary for busy professionals like me. I have written 4 books and I know that as you become more successful, you have access to more people. Your books should give them something to talk about, ponder, and confirm. *This book is fire and as you read it, don't tell Chrissy I told you so! A must-read and then a must-do . . . NOW!!*

Precious Williams
Founder and CEO of Perfect Pitches by Precious LLC,
International Speaker, and Bestselling Author

Delegate Your Book: The Thriving Leaders Guide to Finish Writing the Book Your Industry Needs *is a must-read for all professionals who have dreamed of publishing their own book but can't seem to find the time or have the know-how to make it happen.*

Delegate Your Book *is the solution you have been wishing for. Simple, direct, and effective, this book paves the way for your writing success. A consummate professional, Chrissy Das is the ultimate book whisperer and the writing partner you want on your team. Get her book!*

Diana Long
Master Certified Coach, Facilitator, Mentor Coach

Chrissy has masterfully outlined precisely how to think about and write a business book that will make you shine. She makes it easy for anyone to understand how to start and finish writing a book that has purpose for the reader and that is simultaneously professionally fulfilling for the author. Successful business owners and industry leaders know becoming a published author is the obvious next step in their careers, but if you are stymied, unsure of how to begin or where to go next with your ideas, then the first step is to read Delegate Your Book, *and the second step is to get to writing with Chrissy. Your only regret will be that you didn't do it sooner.*

Bridgett McGowen-Hawkins
Award-Winning International Professional Speaker,
Author, and Publisher

DELEGATE YOUR BOOK

Laure,

Cheers to creating a lasting legacy, my friend!

All the best,

[signature]

DELEGATE YOUR BOOK

The Thriving Leader's Guide to Finish Writing the Book Your Industry Needs

CHRISSY DAS

Nonfiction Ghostwriter

BMcTALKS Press
4980 South Alma School Road
Suite 2-493
Chandler, Arizona 85248

Copyright © 2022 by Chrissy Das. All rights reserved.

Published by BMcTALKS Press, Chandler, Arizona.

No part of this publication may be reproduced, stored in a retrieval system, or transmitted in any form or by any means, electronic, mechanical, photocopying, recording, scanning, or otherwise without the prior written permission of the Publisher. Requests to the Publisher for permissions should be addressed to the Permissions Department, BMcTALKS Press 4980 S. Alma School Rd.; Ste. 2-493, Chandler, AZ 85248 or online at www.bmctalkspress.com/permissions

Limit of Liability/Disclaimer of Warranty: While the publisher and author have used their best efforts in preparing this book, they make no representations or warranties with respect to.the accuracy or completeness of the contents of this book and specifically disclaim any implied warranties or merchantability or fitness for a particular purpose. No warranty may be created or extended by sales representatives or written sales materials. The advice and strategies contained herein may not be suitable for your situation. Neither the publisher nor the author shall be liable for any loss of profit or any other commercial damages, including but not limited to, special, incidental, consequential, or other damages.

FIRST EDITION

Library of Congress Control Number: 2022948000

ISBN: 978-1-953315-24-3

Interior design by Medlar Publishing Solutions Pvt Ltd., India.
Cover design by BMcTALKS Press
Cover photo: Kay Kawada of River Eight & Co

Printed in the United States of America.

This book is dedicated to my husband, Jayant.
Thank you for your love and support. I couldn't have
done this without you as my biggest advocate.

Table of Contents

PART III: The Business of Your Book

Acknowledgments

Thank you to the village of people who made this book possible. First, a huge thank you to Bridgett McGowen-Hawkins and BMcTALKS Press for ushering me through the publishing process. Bridgett, you are my lifeline. My friends, Dr. Pat Baxter, Precious Williams, Li Hayes, Brittney Galagar, and so many others, thank you for bearing witness to the late nights and moments of quiet desperation.

To my ghostwriting colleagues and confidants, thank you to Cindy Tschosik, Thomas Bruein, and Glenn Plaskin. You are titans of the industry, and I love having each one of you on speed dial.

Cory, Steph, and Kimberly, your voices kept me going on the days that I was ready to shelve the project for another day. You each watched out for my mental health in a way that I will never be able to repay.

And finally, my eternal gratitude to Susan Kammeraad-Campbell. Without your glowing introduction to publishing, I never would have found my calling.

A Letter from the Author

Dear Reader,

As a busy leader, you can delegate a lot of things in your life. You know that by focusing on your highest and best use, you are better able to focus on the things that matter most to you. This book will show you how to delegate the parts of writing your book that don't come naturally to your unique talents.

According to data collected by *Publishers Weekly* and Statista, in 2021, more than 1.7 million nonfiction books were launched (either published or self-published) in the United States. Selling a copy of your book (or thousands of copies of it) is a great feeling, but it is not the only source of revenue for a business author, and thankfully so! Those million+ books? The average book sold fewer than 200 copies. You want your book to meet the larger goals you envision for your career, not be another book that will sit on a digital shelf or in a warehouse unread.

I finished writing my first book on behalf of a ghostwriting client in 2015. At last count, I have written more than a dozen books for leaders across service-based industries. It has taken me eight years to prioritize writing my own book for the same reasons my clients have a hard time finishing their own:

- Revenue-generating work fills the calendar
- Time-sensitive business opportunities take priority
- Competing goals of work/play/family/self
- Afraid to move from vision to reality

As a professional ghostwriter, editor, and book coach, I have partnered with more than a hundred authors to help them finish writing the books that their industries need. Some clients run successful service-based businesses; others are conscious creatives who are out to challenge the status quo. Each client has needed to overcome an assortment of obstacles to finish writing their book or hire someone to step in to fill that gap.

You are the only person in the world who can teach your audience about what makes your process work. The lessons you have learned and the hard-won successes you achieved are yours and yours alone. You can choose to share your knowledge and experience with an audience of people who have never met you; they may be interacting with you for the very first time, and this is the only way they can get to know you—this is a weighty thought, but it doesn't have to be a point of paralysis.

Take that first step of knowing what message you want to impart. You'll know you have it right when you can explain the concept to someone outside of your industry and they get it during a two-minute conversation.

You already know what it took to get you to where you are today, but you may not be able to connect all the dots to form a compelling narrative. This is where hiring a professional can come in handy. Just as you wouldn't wire a new outlet for your home office without an electrician, you can make the job of writing a book a lot easier by calling in a trusted expert.

A ghostwriter is a trusted advisor and confidant who will honor the ideas you bring and add some structure and verve to your book. One of my clients shared that they were able to enjoy writing again once they knew that I could take their imperfect manuscript and make it better.

Your book is an extension of your mind, and a ghost-writer is here to help you share your best ideas with an audience that is larger than one you can reach on your own.

Keep writing, and keep reading!!

All the best,

Chrissy Das

Chrissy Das
Nonfiction Ghostwriter

Introduction

As a business leader, you have certain zones of genius where you shine. Think of the pieces in your life that frustrate you or drain your energy; these are the parts that you should delegate to experts who excel in those areas. For example, when I wanted new floors at home, I found the best guy to install them because I knew that I would not be skilled or interested in this task. I viewed samples of his work and spoke with a family who had recently used his services. He did great, and I got to keep my mind focused on running my business.

In *Delegate Your Book: The Thriving Leader's Guide to Finish Writing the Book Your Industry Needs*, I share the different types of experts you can rely on to help you get your book done. If you find yourself at a loss for words, a ghostwriter can step in and help you communicate your ideas into the best words that will resonate with your intended audience. Need some motivation to do it on your own? A book coach is a great person to bring the right blend of structure and creativity to your writing process.

How to Use This Book

You can read this cover-to-cover and glean important points along the way, or you can jump to the section where you are having the most trouble. There are three parts that explain how to write a book. Each of the nine chapters addresses a main idea that will help you in your book-writing journey.

Part I: The Creative Spark sets you up for success with envisioning the type of book you want to write.

Chapter 1 Big Goals, Lasting Legacy gives you the tools you need to imagine the way a book plays a larger role in the goals for your life.

Chapter 2 Find Your Story breaks down the Author's Journey with influence from the late author and professor of literature, Joseph Campbell, and screenwriter, author, and educator, Christopher Vogler.

Chapter 3 Attract Your Audience guides you in identifying who your reader will be and what they are seeking to learn from you.

Part II: The Write Approach shows the different avenues you can pursue so you can finish writing your book with varying levels of support.

Chapter 4 Enjoy Your Voice gives you tools to build the confidence to own your narrative and share your message.

Chapter 5 The Three Main Paths to Writing a Book outlines the specific ways available to help you become an author.

Chapter 6 Common Pitfalls to Avoid cautions against the challenges and obstacles in the writing process whether you go it alone or work with a book coach or ghostwriter.

Part III: The Business of Your Book explains the role a well-themed and well-positioned book can serve in building your professional reputation as well as your business.

Chapter 7 Hire for Talent gives you checklists and best practices for how to hire the right experts to help you finish writing your book.

Chapter 8 Delegate Your Book demonstrates the timeline and tips for success when you are ready to hand off your book to take the next step to finish your manuscript.

Chapter 9 Right Words, Right Time reinforces the impact your book can have when done when you use the right words with the right audience at the right time.

After you read this book, you will have the tools and knowledge you need to make the decision on how you want to finish your book.

Happy reading!

PART I

The Creative Spark

What is it that allows someone to write a book while others wait and plan and move onto other goals? If you have ever wanted to write a book, chances are you were struck by a moment of inspiration and had a message that you wanted to get out into the world. Now, whether you got that message out through a book or if the message stayed trapped in your head, that's another story.

Peter Drucker, author and influencer of corporate culture, writes about "The Discipline of Innovation" in a 2002 issue of *Harvard Business Review*. "In innovation, as in any other endeavor, there is talent, there is ingenuity, and there is knowledge. But when all is said and done, what innovation requires is hard, focused, purposeful work. If diligence, persistence, and commitment are lacking, talent, ingenuity, and knowledge are of no avail."

He makes several good points, namely about going deeper into a single subject to find that catalyst for innovation. If we take a moment and shift from innovation to creativity, we find that Merriam-Webster supports the breakdown of the nuance of innovation (the introduction of something new) as affirmed by creativity (having the quality of something created rather than imitated).

It is my wish for you that you recognize the creative spark within and use it to build the fire that inspires you to share your message with the world.

CHAPTER 1

Big Goals, Lasting Legacy

The person you envision as the "future you" in five, ten years is waiting for you to take the next step in living your optimal life. You have worked hard to get to your current level of success and have put in the time to develop a depth of experience that is unparalleled in your industry. You stand out in your field and still have more to give.

The one commonality among my clients across their many industries and breadth of experiences is the amount of time they have dedicated to become the successful professionals they are now. Even if they are new business owners, they have at least five years in the industry in a hands-on capacity. For the lawyers, they may be shifting from prosecutor to private practice; for REALTORS®, they may be shifting from real estate professional to broker. The ability to identify for yourself what has worked well for you in the past and identify what will take you to that next level is what separates your aspirations from your success. Your book can communicate your process in a way that resonates with future colleagues and clients.

Before you start to write your book, you need to get super clear on the ideal version of yourself you are working towards. Your book will be a reflection of your talents and values; the version of the book is also a version of yourself that you put out in the world forever. You can always update and revise with a future edition—just as you can navigate career changes—but you want to stay as close as possible to your original intent so as not to confuse your readers or your current clients. The goals you set and achieve will help you reach that ideal faster.

Set Your Big Goals

Your book should support your big goals—professional and personal both apply here. Bring the pieces of yourself that you want to amplify, and look for a clear way forward to intersect seemingly unrelated passions.

Those unrelated activities and strengths may have come to the forefront during the pandemic. Post-pandemic, the line between work and home has become blurred more than ever before. More business owners and teams are navigating schedules that allow you to take an exercise class mid-day and log on before or after "traditional office hours" to work at the time when you are most productive or creative. As a result, the divisions between personal and professional matters have fallen into a gray area; this gray area allows business leaders like you to make intentional shifts in how they present themselves. You can bring your own brand of work and your own way to succeed in your industry while allowing aspects of your personality and purpose to peek through.

Professional goals

Professionally, you have a plan that leverages your talents and skills while creating a value for your customer base that is undeniable. Any professional goals you work toward should be supported by the lifestyle you create. If you are expanding your business services to include a new area of expertise, this may be something you want to define in the book. A book gives you the room to explore context around new offerings and gives your reader time to absorb complex information.

You are ready to take major steps toward shaping the career of your dreams, and you have the credentials to back it up. Consider what aspects of your current work situation you would like more of and which ones you would like to minimize or eliminate. While you work on visioning, here are five guiding questions:

1. Which of your clients would you work with again?
2. What made your past client work successful?
3. Who are you excited to work with in the future, and why?
4. What is the most fulfilling part of your day-to-day work?
5. What projects keep getting put on the back burner?

Personal goals

On a personal level, get ready to identify the priorities vital to your current well-being as well as the ones you want to work towards in the long-term. If you want to be home every night with your loved ones, starting a career of in-person training and consulting across the nation is probably not going to help you meet the personal goal of in-person connection with friends and family who are local to you. On the other hand, if you desire to travel more weekends than you are home and you thrive on leading groups, then that in-person training and consulting looks more appealing.

Your personal goals shape the purpose of why you do what you do at work and at home. Double-down on your values and strengths by ensuring that you are in alignment with what you envision as your highest and best use. Consider what aspects of your current personal situation you would like more of and which ones you would like to minimize or eliminate. While you work on visioning, here are five guiding questions:

1. Who in your life do you want to spend more time with?
2. What areas of your life do you want to grow and develop?
3. What areas of your life do you want to minimize or discontinue?
4. What has been your highest personal achievement to date?
5. What do you want to achieve next in your personal life?

There are plenty of books to read and leaders to follow on how to accomplish your goals, but I encourage you to counsel yourself first before seeking an external solution. You have access to everything you need to reach that next level, so take a moment to assess what is going right and what resources you already possess.

Find the intersections to clarify your message

Now that you have envisioned the best version of you—professionally and personally—look for the points of intersecting ideas to become the basis of your book topic. Intersectionality between your personal and professional goals gives you the space to do great things with the biggest impact.

There are no wrong answers when it comes to your professional and personal goals because those are unique to your experience. The book topic should be something that attracts and informs your intended audience. You will want to have a clear audience in mind before you finalize your book topic.

For example, let's say your professional goals are to gain a new certification in your industry so you can add a new service and increase revenue. You will be helping clients by going deeper with your existing clients or expanding your services to a new market of clients. Your personal goals are to travel more, increase visibility, and

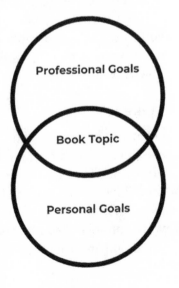

- Gain new certification
- Add new service
- Increase revenue

Position past success to transition to new service

- Travel more
- Increase visibility

build upon the reputation of yourself and your business. The intersection between wanting to travel more and adding a new service will inform your book topic. You will be able to leverage your past success and position yourself to transition to a new service.

When you know what you want to accomplish, you can have fun in the way that you achieve the level of success you envision. Borrow ideas and pathways from people in your network and influencers you follow to make a version that feels right to you. You'll know that you have got it nailed down when it pushes you outside of your comfort zone.

You want that nervous energy that you had when you were a kid and you lost hours doing a creative activity in your zone of genius. Get clear on your goals and how they can help you be even better at your job.

Make it so

Once you have identified your big goals and their intersections, chart a path on the most fun way to get there. Many of my clients are lawyers who have designed their law firms around the way they want to live their lives. Whether you want to run a virtual office where your employees work from anywhere or you value the in-person interactions of a traditional office setup, you get to create the work environment and business you imagine for yourself.

Measure what you want to improve, and make sure that the message of your book will fulfill those metrics in a tangible way.

What Do You Want to Do with Your Legacy?

You have the ability to shape your legacy by magnifying your message. As an individual, you already have influence over your peers and immediate network; as an author, you can generate influence over people you have not yet had the pleasure to meet. Build the legacy you want to outlive your body of work.

Your legacy is the result of you reaching your professional and personal goals. Remember that you can always shift and evolve, so leave room to grow when you are choosing your book topic. The reach of your legacy will be largely determined by the size of the community you build around your expertise.

Who Will Your Legacy Impact?

As authors, we often think of legacy as something literary. What will the critics and colleagues say about my penned tome? It is important that you think more broadly about who your legacy will impact. You have the ability to impact your peers, your loved ones, your clients, your community, and beyond what you can imagine in this moment.

What do you need to do now to start working towards your big goals and planned legacy?

You are a smart and capable person. You already know how to break down your big goals and get the pieces in place to set yourself up for success.

Consider the impact you can have on your community and the people you serve in your business if you are able to communicate your story in a way that magnifies your message. A book that explains your most important message can reach people outside of your network and leave an indelible mark that lasts for decades.

Get clear on your goals and intended legacy and you will be better able to set yourself up for success. To learn more about the topic, books I recommend are listed below.

- *A New Earth: Awakening to Your Life's Purpose* by Eckhart Tolle
- *Designing Your Life: How to Build a Well-Lived, Joyful Life* by Bill Burnett and Dave Evans
- *We: A Manifesto for Women Everywhere* by Gillian Anderson and Jennifer Nadel

CHAPTER 2

Find Your Story

We thrive on stories because they connect us to a shared past and help us explain what we desire in life. Some of my authors have struggled with the idea of how to make nonfiction—a true story—interesting like a fictional story. Enter Joseph Campbell and the well-known Hero's Journey.

The Nonfiction Hero's Journey

Joseph Campbell wrote *The Hero's Journey* in 1949, and its framework has been the basis for most major books and movies since then. The extensive process is a 17-stage journey that takes the main character through Departure, Initiation, and Return. There is literally an entire world within Campbell's thesis, and I recommend studying it as a masterclass in storytelling. For now, I want you to turn your attention to Christopher Vogler. Vogler is best known for his work with Disney, especially the development work he did for the movie *The Lion King*. He adapted Campbell's process in his screenwriting guide, *The Writer's Journey: Mythic Structure for Writers*.

Vogler writes in an article titled "The Memo that Started It All" that "Campbell [...] found that all storytelling, consciously or not, follows the ancient patterns of myth, and that all stories, from the crudest jokes to the highest flights of literature, can be understood in terms of the hero myth; the 'monomyth' [...]." Vogler retells the hero myth in his own way and encourages future writers and screenwriters to do the same.

Three key considerations before we dive into Vogler's 12-step process:

1. The Author as Hero is widely debated within both the writing and marketing communities. Some critics argue it is better to have the Client be the Hero portrayed in the story rather than the subject matter expert as the protagonist. In that vein, I will tell you what many of my lawyer clients tell me: "It depends." I outline the mythic structure below with tie-in to the plot and featured songs of the iconic musical *West Side Story* and explain how to apply it to your nonfiction book with writing prompt options for you to feature either yourself, the Author, or your Client as the Hero.

2. Many nonfiction books follow a 12-chapter outline. You can take this literally (or *literarily*) and use a version of Vogler's process to create your book outline.

3. Another note on the Author as Hero vs. Client as Hero—for the writing prompts, the Author

as Hero will address *you* directly, and Client as Hero will be simplified to *Hero*.

Write to what works, friends. In the well-known stage and screen musical, *West Side Story*, conductor Leonard Bernstein and composer and lyricist Stephen Sondheim, use songs to move the plot forward. Note the order of the songs featured in each of the chapters outlined below; they do not appear in chronological order of the 12 steps in either version of the movie. If you aren't familiar with the musical, check out the 2021 Steven Spielberg remake and the 1961 original. It's definitely worth a watch and a listen to observe the change in nuance and story by simply rearranging the order of the songs.

If you don't have the two and a half hours to watch either movie before you finish reading this book, here is a quick synopsis—*West Side Story* is a love story loosely based on the plot of *Romeo and Juliet*. The Jets are the Montagues, the family backing Tony/Romeo, and The Sharks are the Capulets, the family backing Maria/Juliet. The families in *West Side Story* are teenage gangs formed by Italian immigrants (Jets) and Puerto Rican immigrants (Sharks).

Maria and Tony meet at a neighborhood dance and share a kiss, escalating tensions between the Jets and the Sharks with their star-crossed love. Maria's brother, Bernardo, and Tony's best friend, Riff, schedule a brawl away from the police present at the dance. Anita, Bernardo's girlfriend and Maria's dear friend, tries to convince the boys not to fight. The brawl occurs even as Tony tries to stop it, and in the process, Bernardo dies. In Anita's grief she tells the Jets that Maria is dead because Chino, a Shark who loved her, shot her. Maria is not dead but is in hiding, waiting for Tony to come for her. I'll leave the ending for you to watch, but remember the source material before you get too attached to a happy ending.

Chapter 1: Ordinary World

The reader meets the Hero in their element for the first time. The Hero is at a place of complacency, or minimal comfort, and is unaware that they are about to encounter a significant change. This is a great setup for context of what the Hero's "normal" would be and sets the stage for what is to come. In *West Side Story*, "Jet Song" establishes the baseline of the community and gives a hint at the tensions present in the story as it is just after the first heated exchange between the Sharks and Jets.

Author as Hero: A day in the mundane life of you as the business owner. This is not a time to share a big win or an emotional story; focus on the simple reality of the day-to-day responsibilities of you as the business leader.

- What is your usual day like in your industry?
- What part of your daily routine would surprise your reader?

  Hint: Use the daily routine to give the reader a peek into something larger to come, i.e., the Hero's collective knowledge on a single topic.

Client as Hero: A simple, uninspiring day in the life of the client. This is the perfect chance to show your ideal client that you understand them. You can mention adjacent problems that they might encounter, but it is too early to bring in major problems that you can fix.

- Where is the reader introduced to the Hero?
- What is a daily annoyance that interrupts the Hero's best life?

Hint: The setting is a great opportunity to position the Hero as the Everyman, the ordinary and humble character who serves as a stand-in for the audience to identify directly with that character. Use details that will make the Hero's experience resonate with the reader.

Chapter 2: Call to Adventure

The Hero receives an opportunity for adventure that is too enticing to pass up. This is the moment where they voice their intention to go on the journey. In *West Side Story*, Tony's song, "Something's Coming," spells out this feeling of change. The audience meets him at work and observes as he is pulled toward his destiny.

Author as Hero: Identify the opportunities available to you. This could come in the form of a phone call or message that the reader gets to learn about through your eyes.

- What prompted you to join the industry?
- Did you seek out your industry, or did it seek you out?

Hint: In nonfiction you still have creative license to combine events into a representative sample. If you don't keep a journal, you can go back to your earliest emails with your first clients and reread them for inspiration.

Client as Hero: Identify the opportunities available to your Hero. Introduce the reader to a new idea through a new character, or to move the story forward, explore a new idea with the Hero's inner dialogue.

- What does the Hero want to change in their life?
- Who or what is the Hero seeking, or who or what is seeking the Hero?

Hint: The new character can be the person seeking out the Hero or simply an intermediary. In the case of a new idea instead of a new character, the reader needs to start learning the motivation of the Hero.

Chapter 3: Refusal of the Call

The Hero is reluctant to head into the unknown, though the intention is clear. This is often more of a thinking scene rather than an action one. In *West Side Story*, Tony sings "Maria" after meeting the namesake of the song at the dance and being told by Maria's brother not to pursue her. While the intention of Tony to pursue Maria is clear, there is no action in this scene as he is only thinking about her and not yet actively pursuing her.

Author as Hero: Identify the push and pull of motivations so that the reader understands how you are struggling with the decision to accept or reject the call to adventure.

- What is your hesitation for change?
- What shifts you from inaction to action?

    Hint: This is a good spot to share your vulnerability in an authentic way with your reader.

Client as Hero: Share the motivations of the Hero with the reader so they understand the struggle to accept or reject the call to adventure.

- What does the Hero fear will happen?
- How are they able to move beyond that fear?

    Hint: Adding a level of humanity and vulnerability to the client will make the character more likable to the reader.

Chapter 4: Meeting with the Mentor

Meeting with the Hero's mentor can come in the form of an external person sharing their wisdom. Alternatively, it can be a moment of clarity or reflection where the Hero begins to understand themselves better. Such is the case in the *West Side Story* song "Tonight," sung as a duet between Tony and Maria in secret on her balcony. They share with one another the depth of their affection and the clarity of their relationship. In this instance, they are each serving as the Mentor to the other's Hero.

Author as Hero: Use a moment of internal clarity or reflection to share your growth as a business leader.

- How has self-awareness influenced your thought leadership?
- Describe how you are doing the work to move to the next level.

Hint: Share with the reader the unique way you are overcoming obstacles—your magic bullet.

Client as Hero: As the author, this is an ideal situation to represent your experience and establish yourself as the mentor to the Hero.

- What advice do you give the Hero?
- What tools do you provide so that the Hero is prepared for their journey?

Hint: Guide your Hero with your high-level expertise, not with the details of the plan yet.

Chapter 5: Crossing the First Threshold

The story begins to pick up pace here with the first intentional actions of the Hero. In *West Side Story*, the orchestration for "The Dance at the Gym Mambo" lends emotion and nuance to the actions of each of the main characters. The dance is the moment the Hero is crossing the first threshold. Both the Jets and the Sharks act intentionally to begin planning, The Rumble, a foreshadowing of the action that will follow.

Author as Hero: Teach the reader the first step of your process. Describe the first action you take to enact your expertise.

- What is the first action in your process?
- Describe a small result of the first action step.

   Hint: This chapter is a balance between action and microsresult. You want a win here but a small one.

Client as Hero: The Hero takes the first step in working with you. Describe the first action you take together.

- What is the first step the Hero takes?
- What are some immediate changes from the first shift in behavior?

   Hint: Use a strong start. Now is not the time to be subtle.

Chapter 6: Tests, Allies, and Enemies

The Hero meets allies and enemies or encounters tests. This is a proving ground for the reader to learn the big obstacles that the Hero is up against. In *West Side Story*, the Jets name one of their biggest foes and detail the societal obstacles that exist for them in this new world in the song "Gee, Officer Krupke." This is one of the songs written by Sondheim, and the lyrics give a pretty extensive list of everything that can go wrong in the lives of the Jets.

Author as Hero: Focus on the training you undergo that builds your expertise. Forces, both internal and external, arise to block your way, but there is still a clear path forward.

- What are you fighting against?
- Who is an ally that can help you overcome external obstacles?

    Hint: This can be a serious chapter, but make sure to have a moment of levity to keep your reader engaged.

Client as Hero: The Hero is tested, and the reader is introduced to enemies and allies. The test can be planned or unexpected—be intentional in your choice.

- What external obstacles is the Hero up against?
- What allies are available to step in and lend a hand?

    Hint: You can use this chapter to introduce the Hero to a secondary resource that can help them in their journey. (You shouldn't be both the mentor and the ally.)

Chapter 7: Approach to the Innermost Cave

The object of the quest is hidden in a dangerous place, historically underground. In *West Side Story*, the innermost cave is the inner thoughts of the main characters. During "Tonight Quintet," Tony, Maria, Bernardo, Anita, and Riff prepare for The Rumble between the Jets and Sharks.

Each character is focused on their own motivations, and the scene is an excellent microcosm of the larger story.

Author as Hero: Emotions are high before the big ordeal. Share what you are feeling with the reader so they understand the tensions at play.

- What is the deep work you need to do to prepare for the big event?
- Think about the last time you approached a task with renewed confidence.

  Hint: You can use this chapter as a flashback to foreshadow the strength you will need to overcome The Ordeal.

Client as Hero: The purpose of the Hero's journey is revealed. The Hero faces their greatest danger before reaching the summit.

- Give the Hero an outlet for their emotions through dialogue or a monologue.
- When did the Hero face similar issues before?

  Hint: The Hero will need to communicate to the reader their own self-awareness of their journey.

Chapter 8: The Ordeal

This is the moment in the story when the Hero faces their biggest challenge. The reader is left uncertain if the Hero will be successful in their mission. In *West Side Story*, after the violence of the Rumble between the Jets and the Sharks, Maria and Anita meet. Anita sings

"A Boy Like That" to explain that Tony murdered Maria's brother and will cause Maria further harm if she stays loyal to him. This is the lowest point for Anita as her lover has just been murdered. (This song also foreshadows Anita being attacked by the Jets in a future scene.)

Author as Hero: This is the low point in your journey. You face the hardest struggle of your career.

- What is a pivotal moment in your career that would resonate with your reader?
- Describe the impact on your life from your experience during this time in your career.

  Hint: If a specific moment doesn't come to mind, search through old journals, calendars, and emails for verbiage and events to jog your memory.

Client as Hero: The Hero has to fight to make it through this tough situation. They are unsure if they will get through unscathed.

- How does the Hero react to the tough situation?
- What is the harm that could befall them if things go wrong?

  Hint: Think of the client stories you have heard. Which ones stand out to you years later?

Chapter 9: Reward

The Hero receives a moment of reconciliation or settles a conflict, relieving the tension created by The Ordeal.

In *West Side Story*, Maria sings "I Have a Love" as a reply to Anita's "A Boy Like That," and their interchange is gut-wrenching for the audience. Both women have a deeper understanding of the world because of their experience during The Ordeal.

Author as Hero: You get closure or relief in what you were working toward. You earn a certification or recognition in your industry.

- Which of your accomplishments do you want to highlight?
- How does the recognition of your achievement play into your story as an expert in your industry?

Client as Hero: The Hero achieves their goal. This is a moment of celebration you can share with them.

- Which goal does the Hero achieve?
- What is the larger meaning behind their win?

Chapter 10: The Road Back

The Hero finds a moment of quiet and reflection before the weight of the world comes crashing back down. In *West Side Story*, Tony and Maria share a duet in "One Hand, One Heart" as a pseudo wedding. The music and lyrics reinforce the social rituals that show how their life could be if their relationship could exist outside of their current situation.

Author as Hero: Your story isn't over. Challenges you face in business continue to surface, but the message is one of optimism.

- What is the new challenge you face?
- What gives you energy to keep going?

Client as Hero: The Hero is aware of the challenges still to come, though the worst of it is over. They have a renewed energy and resilience.

- Describe the Hero's understanding of the next challenges to come.
- What gives the Hero energy to keep going?

Chapter 11: The Resurrection

The Hero is transformed from the experience and knowledge they gained in their journey. This moment takes the Hero out of the special world of their journey and positions them back within the ordinary world. In *West Side Story*, Valentina sings "Somewhere" with lyrics that hearken to the resurrection of relationships in a calmer, safer world.

Author as Hero: Your moment of transformation does not come without pain. Share a similarly intense low point as in Chapter 8: The Ordeal.

- What is your point of transformation?
- How does your inner change impact the way you do business?

Client as Hero: This is often a replay of the intense emotions in The Ordeal. The Hero faces a transformational experience.

- Did the Hero's worst fear come true?
- What transformation is the Hero facing?

Chapter 12: Return with the Elixir

The Hero returns to the ordinary world transformed by their journey in a celebration of triumph or moment of healing. This scene is often paired with a tangible treasure or a lesson learned. In *West Side Story*, the instrumentals in "Finale" give the mournful backdrop of Maria calling for a cease in fighting between the Sharks and the Jets.

Author as Hero: The conclusion of the book encapsulates the end result of the big transformation. Your reader should have a thorough understanding of your expertise and the results you can provide.

- What is the call to action that you issue to the reader?
- What is the feeling you want to leave the reader as they absorb the lesson?

  Hint: At the end of the book, you will want to present a call-to-action for the reader to take, such as a link to a website for them to read more about your services. Ideally, the book will feed into a direct service or product.

Client as Hero: The Hero emerges changed for the better from the journey. The reader should feel satisfied and have a desire to start their own journey.

- How has the journey changed the Hero's story?
- Is the Hero feeling triumphant or pensive?

Hint: Remind the reader how they can replicate the success of the client and provide a call-to-action.

What's Your Story?

"The myth is infinitely flexible,
capable of endless variation
without sacrificing any of its magic,
and it will outlive us all."

Christopher Vogler

How will you tell your story? Are you the hero or the mentor in your ideal scenario? The way you share the information with your audience should be a direct correlation to the way you want to work with them. If you are a visionary with big ideas and ideals, you are more likely to be portrayed as the mentor; if you are an everyman who has been where your reader is now and you want to keep them from the same obstacles you had to overcome, you could position yourself as an approachable hero.

Brené Brown's book, *Rising Strong*, guides you through how to talk about your vulnerabilities and moments of adversity. The more authentic you can be with yourself, the more of your story you will be able to share with your readers. Whatever path you decide to follow in telling your story, commit fully to the method.

Your perspective and experience are what each of your readers signed up to follow. Bring them along for the journey, and make their time with you well spent.

Read more to learn the best ways to tell your story. Some books to get you started are listed below.

- *The Hero with a Thousand Faces* by Joseph Campbell
- *The Writer's Journey: Mythic Structure for Writers* by Christopher Vogler
- *Rising Strong* by Brené Brown

CHAPTER 3

Attract Your Audience

Your reader is eagerly waiting for you to finish writing your book. They want to learn everything they can from you, and you want a format where your message can transform from one-to-one to one-to-many. Even if you are not a professional speaker, think about who would come to hear you speak. The same audience who would fill a venue to hear you impart your advice is the same group of people who will make up your readers.

Identify Your Ideal Reader

Who will read your nonfiction book? Learn as much as you can about them. In marketing, the word used to describe a "representative" person is "avatar." The more detailed you can make your avatar's preferences, educational background, income level, interests, and reading habits, the more tailored you can make the content of your book. Some details to consider include the following:

- What is your reader's profession?
- What is your reader's income?
- What is their level of education?
- What are their interests?
- How often does your reader pick up a book?
- Do they listen to audiobooks?

Take your cues from the pieces of information that are in common with your ideal clients, and share your message like you are having a conversation with that person. The depth of your conversation will depend on the type of book you want to share with your audience and the type of action you want the reader to take.

Identify the Desired Action

How will your reader react when they read some (or all) of your book? What ideas within the book will prompt them to take action? How can you guide them toward the action you desire they take? Are you explaining innovative industry processes to your peers so they can grow and build in the same way that you have? Are you breaking down concepts to educate your clients? I'll give you a hint: the best book will not do both. You will want to pick a lane and follow that narrative through to the desired conclusion.

If you are going for the innovative industry narrative, you are likely writing to an audience of your peers. Feel free to drop in the jargon and industry-speak that make you sound like an insider. Beware of creating an echo chamber, and instead, bring in your fresh perspective.

You know what has worked for your business to date, and you want to share that information with others who will benefit from your been there, done that example.

If you are educating clients, meet them at their current level of knowledge and layer in your expertise. You can make the journey to their goal effortless and enjoyable as you guide them on what works and what doesn't. In this instance, you avoid heavy technical terms and unexplained jargon. Instead, give your reader easy wins to build their confidence and tools and exercises to help them along their journey.

Build the Audience You Envision

You are never starting from scratch when you are building your community of readers. As an influencer in your community and an expert in your field, you have access to the minds of the people in your network. Now, your entire network is not necessarily your target audience, but there will be people and groups within your network who will be supporters of your work. Increase your visibility while you are working on your book so that you have a built-in community ready to support your book promotion and your next steps in business.

A quick note on increasing your visibility before your book idea is fully formed: Don't tell everyone you are working on writing a book. Build the community based on your general knowledge and interests without making a formal announcement that you are writing a book. This will allow you to build your confidence in the project before sharing it with the public.

7 Ways to Build a Community of Readers Pre-Book Launch

1. **Set up your profile on LinkedIn.**
   Position yourself in a way that showcases the depth of your experience in your industry. Start connecting with colleagues and peers in your industry. If this is your first book, I do not advise including "author" in your title or headline. Wait until the book is published.

2. **Attend local and virtual conferences that will attract your target audience of readers.**
   For example, if you are a real estate professional, you may want to attend events that provide value and resources to families. An estate planning attorney may want to attend conferences that attract retirees.

3. **Join a professional development organization.**
   A quick Google search will let you know about the options specific to your industry. A wider net to cast would be memberships in organizations like Toastmasters and Business Network International (BNI) where the attendees are interested in personal growth or business networking.

4. **Claim your author profiles on all the social media platforms.**
   You may want to avoid creating the full profile just yet, but go ahead and claim your username. If you have a common name, a variation is fine as long as you are consistent across platforms.

Two possible variations are FirstNameLast-NameAuthor or FirstNameLastNameIndustry.

5. **Purchase a domain or two.**

Buy YourName.com through your preferred domain provider. I recommend domains.google.com if you are unsure where to start. If your name is already taken, purchase the same domain name as the username you chose for your author profiles on social media.

(A few notes on domains: You can forward YourName.com to your LinkedIn profile if/until you are ready to launch a specific website. You can also purchase the domain for your intended book title, but I encourage you to get further in the writing process before doing so because your title can change.)

6. **Designate two or three friends to share your dream of writing a book.**

When you share the news with your trusted circle, you build your confidence in the project in a contained way. It is okay to share your book writing journey with whomever you choose, but I encourage you to put in the work before making your plan public.

7. **Start a LinkedIn newsletter about your area of expertise.**

Begin by writing three or four articles before officially launching so you can continue publishing at a steady pace. Depending on the size of your existing LinkedIn network, it may take several issues before your newsletter gains much attention. Keep it going for at least six months before you decide whether to increase or decrease how frequently you publish.

Your audience will wait for you until you are ready to publish, but remember that they won't wait forever. Do your research and keep creating content while you pursue the larger goal of your book. Try to avoid getting stuck in the minutiae of what you need to make this book successful. Focus on providing value to your readers.

To learn more about positioning for your audience, books I recommend are listed below.

- *Bad Bitches and Power Pitches* by Precious Williams
- *The Storytelling Edge* by Shane Snow and Joe Lazauskas
- *Youtility: Why Smart Marketing is About Help Not Hype* by Jay Baer

PART II

The Write Approach

The write approach builds on the creative spark because once you have an idea for a book, you're going to want to get that out in the world as soon as possible. Have you ever gotten stuck in perfection paralysis? You should know there is no right or wrong way to get your book done. The right approach to "the write approach" is to do it until it gets done. If you are able to do that solo, that's awesome; if you need some support, then know that there are many ways to work with experts to get your book done.

Focus on finding the right person. With the right approach, that right person will show you how to finish writing your book in a way that is aligned with your personal and professional goals. Pay attention to the tasks that are easy for you and the things that are hard for you. So, if something is too difficult, you want to pass that off to someone who can do it better and faster, so you can stick to your core competencies.

CHAPTER 4

Enjoy Your Voice

You are uniquely positioned to tell your story because of your life experience, business knowledge, and success to date. Savor the ability to share your wisdom with others. Identify the words that resonate for you and build on those to make your message known in a style that is wholly yours.

Audit Your Public Persona

What is the message that your audience associates with you and your business? Start by doing a Google search for your name and analyze the first three pages of results. Check for alternate spellings of your name, and set up a Google Alert to stay in the loop on any changes to your search results. If the most popular pages are not in sync with your current story, it's time to shift your positioning to a message that aligns with your intended path.

Define Your Narrative

Choose the story you want to tell about your business. Which aspect of your experience do you focus on? Where do you fast-forward and jump ahead to change the scene? Pay attention to the story that you tell yourself and that you hear yourself telling others. Words have power, and there may be a subconscious reason that you choose to explain yourself in the way that you do.

Hone Your Tone

During the audit of your public persona, you will also want to track the types of content you share on social media. Are your posts in sync with the message you are trying to communicate to your audience? For the posts that receive a lot of engagement, what are you doing differently? Double-down on what works for your audience. They want to get to know you and your material better.

The better you understand your motivation and message, the easier it will be for you to communicate it to your audience.

To learn more about the best ways to tell your story, books I recommend are listed below.

- *Say It Well: Creating and Tailoring Value-Driven Communication* by Derek Lott
- *Speak: Find Your Voice, Trust Your Gut, and Get From Where You Are to Where You Want to Be* by Tunde Oyeneyin
- *The Creative Habit: Learn It and Use It for Life* by Twyla Tharp

CHAPTER 5

The Three Main Paths to Writing a Book

Writing a book is hard work, but it has been done hundreds of thousands of times before you picked up your pen. The simplicity in putting your words on record is calming, and seeing the finished product can be rewarding both from an esoteric and financial position.

There are three main paths to writing a book; like any option, the hypothetical is always going to be a small step away from the reality. Follow the option that makes the most sense for your situation, and be willing to pivot if your situation changes.

Write It Yourself

There's something extremely satisfying about completing a project all on your own. Whether it's client work or building a deck in the backyard, doing it solo is an attractive proposition because you are in control from start to finish. Doing it yourself can also save you quite a bit of money.

Writing retreat

You can sign up for a weekend writing workshop and crank out a good chunk of your book if you have the dedicated time and talent to do so. For your first book, this might be too immersive to be comfortable. If you are interested in this route, consider booking a staycation and seeing how many chapters you can get through without any distractions.

Between other responsibilities

If you wait until the perfect time to write your book, you are probably not going to get around to doing it this year. There will always be something else that you could or should be doing, and it doesn't involve typing away for hours. You can make this method work for you if you have a consistent schedule or a really good support system to help you coordinate the other non-book responsibilities.

Best-case scenario

You write the book of your dreams in less than six months and are ready to submit it to your publisher. You have saved some money by forgoing a book coach or ghostwriter and can now put that money towards your book launch.

Hire a Book Coach

All of the greats have coaches to make them better at what they want to excel in. Athletes and actors have coaches who specialize in creating success within their industries. The coach's role is to support the talented person in reaching an even higher level of potential than they could on their own. Now with a book coach, the same is true for writers who are probably already pretty great at what they do but they just need an extra level of support.

If you have a lot of fear and insecurity around writing, a book coach can help you elevate your style and improve your writing with different types of approaches. Look for one who specializes in where you need the most help. For example, I am a book coach who also is a professional editor. As a professional editor, I'm trained to watch for grammar, punctuation, syntax, style—all of the elements that will make your book stronger.

I bring that hat to my book coaching session because I find it to be really engaging to the author when they have their own work they can refer back to. In some book coaching instances, you are going to go through their process or their workbook. That type of structure is great if that's what you're looking for.

When you are looking for a book coach, think about how you want to be supported. Do you want voice-mail and text support? Do you want them to meet you in-person? Do you want them to meet you on Zoom? How often do you want to meet them?

How often should you meet?

I would suggest no less than once a month. You will want to be able to see the needle move as you work toward finishing your book. And if you're meeting once a quarter, then that gives you a lot of time to wait and see. When you're working on a book—or when you're working on any project really—you are going to fill the amount of time that you allow yourself to get things done.

If you give yourself a year to write a book, which is fine—that's a good amount of time to write a book—you'll likely finish the book within that year. If you give yourself six months to write the same book, it is possible you could do it in six months. It's all a matter of syncing your calendar to the level of success that you want. And it's extremely possible. I've had coaching clients meet with me once a week for a few months, then at the six-month mark, they meet me twice a week just to wrap that project. Now, one of the things about working with the book coach who's also a writing coach is that you're going to see improvement in all the types of writing you need to do.

How long is each session?

Each book coaching session is approximately 45 minutes to an hour in length. But you can also do marathon sessions. Maybe you're working on more than one chapter or an outline for a new book. You could go as long as the book coach allows. I've had some book coaching sessions that lasted up to three hours. It just depends on your energy level and your coach's energy level as well as the depth of the material that you're going over.

Stay flexible and stay communicative. The more clearly you communicate to your book coach what you want, the more readily they'll be able to help you meet those goals. Book coaches are magical, but we're not mind readers. In order to make sure your needs are being met, clearly communicate those needs.

Best-case scenario

The best-case scenario in working with a book coach is that you get your book done on time. You get your book out of your head and onto the page for a fraction of the cost of working with a ghostwriter because the ghostwriter transforms your ideas into the book that you envision. Your book coach is really there to support you in your own writing practice. If you're planning on building your writing habit, then a book coach is definitely the way to go.

Hire a Ghostwriter

A ghostwriter is a trusted advisor and confidant who will honor the ideas you bring and add some structure and verve to your book. One of my clients shared, "Chrissy has a unique way of drawing you into her world with her skills of writing and storytelling." They were able to enjoy writing again once they knew that I could take their imperfect manuscript and make it better.

Your book is an extension of your mind, and a ghostwriter is here to help you share your best ideas with a larger audience than you can reach on your own.

When to start working together?

You start working with a ghostwriter after you have a very clear idea of what you want your book to be about and who you're writing it for. It's not advisable to start working with a ghostwriter before those two things are fleshed out because you're investing a significant amount of time and money in making this book happen.

You want the manuscript to be finished in the smoothest way possible because you want to put a quality book out.

The best way to put a quality book out into the world is to do the project in an intentional way. Engage a ghost-writer when you have a clear idea for your book and a clear scope of project. So, you will want to know what you're writing, an estimate of how long the book will be, and your timeline for publication. If you're going the traditional publishing route, you probably need to finish the book approximately a year in advance. But if you're going for an indie or hybrid publisher, then five months or six months is usually enough time to get to market. For the people interested in self-publishing, that really just depends on how quickly you can project manage the publishing process and the turnaround time for each of your vendors.

What to expect?

The ghostwriter will send you an intake form with a list of questions to get you thinking about the themes in your book. Often you will work together on a smaller project before beginning a full-length book. Some ghostwriters will offer a writing sample or compatibility assessment to make sure that the project is a good fit. Once you get started, the ghostwriter will usually interview you at the beginning of the engagement, and they may send a couple of follow-up emails; but in general, they will be working from the source material that you provide.

Ghostwriting can also be more collaborative. The ghostwriter is going to do some chapters on their own and wait for your feedback, and then other chapters may be more heavily involved. By "heavily involved," that could look like you providing multiple interviews or you submitting additional writing samples. All options are valid. Make sure you are clear on the scope of work so that, again, your needs are met and clearly communicated.

Best-case scenario

The best-case scenario when working with a ghostwriter is that you forget which words they came up with and which ones you suggested. The finished product should be so seamlessly bound and sound enough like you that clients, your parents, and your peers believe that you wrote this book. Your book is a manifestation of your ideas so, of course, it should sound like the authentic version of you.

CHAPTER 6

Common Pitfalls to Avoid

Writing a nonfiction book is both a science and an art. You want to control for the variables that you can while allowing room for spontaneity. It can be a delicate balance and, depending on the chapter you are focused on, can swing from one extreme to the other. You have choices at every stage of the writing process; knowing your options can be a powerful motivator to help you get it done no matter the obstacles.

In Chapter 5, you learned the three main paths to writing a book:

1. Go it alone by writing the book yourself.
2. Write the book with the support of a book coach.
3. Work with a ghostwriter to get the book finished.

There are unique pitfalls for each path you choose, and you can prepare to overcome them if you have insight into the process.

Pitfalls to Avoid When Going It Alone

Some authors have the time and talent to get their manuscript to the finish line on their own. This is a good option if writing your books is something you have dreamed of for a long time and you are comfortable with your writing voice.

If you're going to write your book alone, here are some common pitfalls to avoid and what to do instead:

Avoid talking about the book before you have written more than half of the manuscript.

It can be tempting to shout it from the rooftops that you are going to be an Author with a capital "A"— a word of caution before you take out a billboard downtown or start running ads on social media ... you need to pause. Take a deep breath before you share your story idea with the masses because you need time to solidify your intent and home in on your purpose, which brings me to the next pitfall to avoid ...

Avoid writing without a clear purpose.

Start with the end in mind. The old adage is said so often because it is necessary. You are about to take on a large project; do it with the end in mind so it serves your larger purpose. A book is going to look great on your shelf and can be a wonderful outlet for organizing your body of work. Use it to get what you want on a larger scale. Build your speaking or consulting career, or use it to transition from one industry to another.

Avoid taking on more than is reasonable with your current workload.

You are a busy professional. Between work, social, and community involvement, you already have a full calendar. What are the big deadlines and commitments you have coming up in the next six to twelve months? Be mindful of your availability, and leave time for fun with friends and family. Writing a book can be its own kind of fun, especially when you are pouring your ideas onto the page without a frenzied rush to the finish line.

Avoid unrealistic deadlines.

Deadlines, even self-imposed ones, can bite you in the butt. You set yourself up for failure if you don't allot a reasonable amount of time to take care of what you need to get done. It can be extremely damaging to your mindset when your goals remain unmet. Set reasonable goals, then increase them as you build your writing muscles.

Three Ways to Succeed When Going It Alone

1. **Double-down on your strengths.**
    Going solo means your self-awareness needs to be on point. The clearer you are on your strengths, the more you can leverage them to help you reach your goal. Instead of trying to improve your weaknesses, spend more time using your strengths to make progress.

2. **Keep your priorities in order.**
   You are writing your book ideally with a singular goal in mind. Focus on achieving that goal while still keeping up with your other professional and personal priorities.
3. **Set a reasonable pace.**
   Be kind to yourself as you work to meet your deadlines. If you aren't used to writing more than 1,000 words in a day, start with 500-word writing sessions and time yourself to establish a baseline before you plan the whole timeline for completing your manuscript.

Pitfalls to Avoid When Hiring a Book Coach

Are you ready to write but are nervous that perfectionism will keep you from ever finishing? A book coach can help you meet your writing goal if you avoid the following pitfalls.

Avoid talking about the book before you have written more than half of the manuscript.

You are going to be excited when you start working with your book coach. Give it some time before you share outside your inner circle. You don't have to write half of the manuscript on your own. In fact, you can probably find a good book coach after completing only a chapter or two.

Avoid writing without a clear purpose.

Stay focused on your writing goal so you maximize your time with the book coach. One of the perks of using a book coach is that you can plan out your writing sessions, knowing you have the support you need to keep moving forward.

Avoid taking on more than is reasonable with your current workload.

Plan your next steps before taking the first one. Your book should support your other business and life goals rather than being crammed in between other accomplishments. Your book coach will support you in the way that you need by meeting you where you are. Be honest with yourself about where you are and what you can realistically do.

Avoid unrealistic deadlines.

Schedule your book coaching sessions at a frequency that works well with your schedule. You want enough time to prepare material for your next chapter or section before you meet with them again. It can be tempting to cram in multiple sessions and accelerate, but steady wins the race.

Avoid getting stuck in the minutiae.

There is a reason you chose the book coach you hired, and each coach's process will be a little different. If you know how you like to work, find someone who is a great fit for the style of support you need. Do your due diligence at the beginning of the project rather than questioning the how in the middle. Don't be afraid to ask questions if a situation arises that feels uncomfortable, but clear communication between the author and the book coach is vital to a successful project, reducing the likelihood of sticky situations arising.

Three Ways to Succeed When Hiring a Book Coach

1. **Hire the best fit for your writing style.**
   You will spend a lot of time with your book coach, so you will want to make sure that the process of working together will be enjoyable. Start with a sample chapter to see if the results from working together match the writing style you envision for your book.
2. **Hire a book coach who specializes in your genre.**
   There are hundreds of talented book coaches out there. You will want to choose the one who has written books in your genre. They need to know what the publisher is looking for and, more importantly, which words and phrases will connect with your intended reader.
3. **Follow your chosen book coach's process.**
   Each book coach brings their own skillset and training to the session. Once you have vetted them and started working together, be consistent in following their suggested process. They do this professionally and want you to succeed.

Pitfalls to Avoid When Working with a Ghostwriter

Some authors may want a helping hand on some or all their chapters. If you plan to work with a ghostwriter, here are some common pitfalls to avoid.

Avoid talking about the book before you have written more than half of the manuscript.

Yes, you will still want to keep the news of your book under wraps before you are ready to make a grand announcement. When you are interviewing ghostwriters, share your general idea for the book, but don't give away your intellectual property on the first call. When you have narrowed it down to one or two ghostwriters, have them sign a nondisclosure agreement (NDA) before having them review any of your material.

Avoid writing without a clear purpose.

You want to work smarter, not harder. The difference in writing with a clear purpose on your own is that you know what is in your head. Try to avoid starting the writing process with a ghostwriter without having a clear outline and plan for the finished book.

Avoid taking on more than is reasonable with your current workload.

A professional ghostwriter will have a plan in place, complete with an estimated timeline, on your next steps. But from your side also, set clear expectations on your availability for interviews and other actionable items.

Avoid unrealistic deadlines.

If you want to launch the book on a certain date, allow plenty of buffer time for incidental situations. Your ghostwriter should lead the date of deliverables and stick to it as much as possible. Make the process easier for both of you by holding up your end of the bargain.

If you agree to send revisions within a week of receiving a chapter, schedule time in your calendar to review the chapter and send in your notes by the expected time.

Avoid getting stuck in the minutiae.

There is a reason that you chose the ghostwriter you hired. Let them carry out the project in the way they know how. Each ghostwriter's process will be a little different, but do your due diligence at the beginning of the project rather than questioning the how in the middle. Don't be afraid to ask questions if a situation arises that feels uncomfortable, but clear communication between the author and the ghostwriter is vital to a successful project.

Three Ways to Succeed When Working with a Ghostwriter

1. **Ask for what you want.**
    Be as specific as possible in the goals you have for the book. You'll want to establish details like length, audience, and tone; beyond the structure of the book, you will need an end goal that the book will help you achieve.
2. **Offer as much information as possible.**
    You are an expert on your topic, and the ghostwriter is an expert at writing. Give the ghostwriter as much information as you can so that your book is fully developed and personal to your story.

3. **Provide clear feedback.**
   There will be milestones as you work with your ghostwriter. Provide clear feedback early and often so that you can efficiently receive the best version of your book.

It's Not So Scary

There are a lot of ways the writing process can go wrong, but there are so many ways it can go right. Commit to yourself to follow-through on your chosen path, and give it time to all come together. Do your homework and ask for references and samples. Be kind to yourself, and invest the resources necessary to make your vision a reality. With the right support and mindset, you will be able to overcome the pitfalls and get your book out into the world with as much fanfare as you desire!

PART III

The Business
of Your Book

The Creative Spark spurred you to action and The Write Approach helped you create a plan to finish your book. The Business of Your Book is where you're really going to break down the tangibles of this project.

What is your ROI? What is the amount of time and money that you need to invest to get this project done? And what is going to be your return on that investment? When you choose the right topic for your business book, you will be able to leverage your intellectual property to attract an audience that is revenue-generating for you. Now, the way that the revenue is generated may look different for you than for another author.

For example, if you are a lawyer, and you are writing a book to encourage the lawyers in the industry, then your return on investment for your book might look like building out a course around your book's content. In that case, you're going to want to look at all of the costs for building out the course in addition to finishing the book. And so, for that, reverse engineer the success that you want.

CHAPTER 7

Hire for Talent

As a business leader, you know what it is like to negotiate rates on behalf of your department or your company. We all want to get the best value and feel like we got a good deal for the amount of money we put into a project. When budgeting for a large project such as finishing the manuscript for your next business book, it is important to consider several key aspects:

- What is the amount of money you can allocate to the project?
- What is the amount of time you can allocate to the project?
- What is the return on time and money that you are expecting from your investment?

A conservative estimate for the average billable hourly rate for a business professional in 2022 is $150. Now, for my lawyer friends getting away from billable hours, think of this as your blended rate. The amount of money you can allocate to the project is variable depending on your actual rates and the current level of profit your business is generating.

Your current client rates and the level of profit your business is generating also have a direct impact on the amount of time you can allocate to the project. Whether you are experiencing feast or famine in your business, the hours in each day can stretch only so far. When business is too busy, it can require a disproportionate amount of your time; when business is too slow, the extra time can feel like a gift but not at the expense of the added stress of making payroll.

The high point in all of this is that when business does better, you can delegate more to free up your time and make more money.

If you find a ghostwriter who will work hourly instead of on a project basis, you still need to calculate the value of having a true professional craft the chapter you envision. For example, a professional writer is going to have a better handle on what the publisher is looking for and what trends readers are expecting to see. If you've ever tried to cut your own hair, you know the benefit of relying on an expert to carry out that skilled task.

My authors know that the investment they make in their book is an investment in their brand and their credibility, and they do not expect a direct ROI from book sales to recoup the cost of creating the manuscript. Additional costs to launch the book will include publishing and marketing as well as any collateral materials you want like bookmarks, postcards, or pens. Focus your resources where they will do the most to help you meet your larger goals. If you are planning to sell the book, consider the ways you will leverage your story in addition to the baseline price of the book itself.

What's a Single Book Sale Worth?

A single book sale is worth more than the few dollars you will make selling a copy. Calculate instead what a new client, consulting project, or speaking gig will add to your bottom line. If your average client value is four- or five-figures, then it may make sense for you to invest more in your book up front.

What are Bulk Book Sales Worth?

Anytime you sell ten or more books in a single transaction, that sale is considered a bulk book sale. Bulk book sales can happen at speaking events, conferences, and trainings. Your take home for the sale per book will be less than it is for single sales, but you can use the sale as a great opportunity for a photo op—if you personally autograph the books and mail the box, shoot a prep reel. When you supply bulk for an in-person event, be sure to have a photographer assigned to shoot some photos at the author signing table.

Who to Hire?

Your clients hire you because they know you are knowledgeable about your industry, and you follow-through with great work. Use the same avenues that your clients use to find you to locate the expert you need to help you succeed in your vision for writing a business book.

Where to Find a Book Coach?

You can find a book coach by asking authors whose books you enjoyed if they worked with a book coach to get their book done. This is much more acceptable than asking for an introduction to an author's agent. A happy author will usually be delighted to share their book coach.

If you already have a publisher in mind as part of your book plan, reach out to them to ask if they have any book coaches they recommend. Be as specific as possible in describing how you like to work so that the publisher can make the best recommendation for you.

How to Vet a Book Coach?

Book coaching is not a regulated industry. You will find coaches with a wide range of experiences and skillsets. You will want to find the one whose style and process will help you reach the goal you have for your book.

Below is a list of ten questions to ask a potential book coach about your nonfiction business book:

1. What is your professional background?
2. How many authors have you coached?
3. How long did it take them to finish their books?
4. What references and links to a representative sample of your past work with authors are you able to share with me?
5. What can I expect during a book coaching session?
6. What is the cost per session? Do you have a flat rate option?

7. How do I schedule a session with you?
8. What is your cancellation policy if I have a last-minute scheduling conflict?
9. Can I contact you between sessions with additional questions?
10. How much pre-work do you expect me to bring to each session?

If you are unsure how to pick between your top two, ask if they would be willing to do an hourly rate for a single sample session.

Where to Find a Ghostwriter?

You'll find potential ghostwriters through trusted colleagues and advisors. So, for example, if you have a plan to write a business book and you already know which publisher you'd like to work with, reach out and ask them for recommendations on who they've worked with before and who they would recommend. Another way to start your search for a ghostwriter is to ask your friends who've written books if they worked with a ghostwriter or book coach.

How to Vet a Ghostwriter?

When you reach the vetting process of your ghostwriter, you will want to make sure that they specialize in writing for the target audience you are addressing. For example, a memoir ghostwriter might not be the best fit for a business book. You will also want to know how many books they have written and how many books they work on at a time.

It's possible the ghostwriter won't be able to show you their full list of books, but they should have a robust list of references. When you're checking the references for a ghostwriter, ask questions like:

- How long have you known the ghostwriter?
- Have you worked with the ghostwriter directly, or have you worked on similar projects together?
- What do you consider to be the strength of this ghostwriter, and what do you consider to be some of the challenges in working together?
- Do you have a long-term relationship with the ghostwriter?

Answers to these questions are going to indicate if the ghostwriter is consistent and whether the author can be reasonably assured that the ghostwriter will do a good job.

The ghostwriting process is extremely creative. Within that, there's always some play on how the project gets done. For instance, you might ask your ghostwriter "How do you like working? What success have your authors found in working with you?"

Below is a list of ten questions to ask a potential ghostwriter about your nonfiction business book:

1. What is your writing experience?
2. What topics do you specialize in?
3. What references are you able to share with me?
4. May I see an example of your writing style?

5. How many authors have you ghostwritten books for? Do you have any repeat clients?
6. How long does it take you to finish writing a book?
7. What is it like to work with you?
8. How will we communicate about the project?
9. How much pre-work do you expect me to do before you begin writing?
10. What is your cancellation policy if I change my mind about the topic?

My ghostwriting process is customized for each of my authors. I have a baseline of information from the author that I need, but the way I get that information varies from client to client. It could be through interviewing, analyzing existing content, or doing supplemental research. The author has a certain number of chapters in mind for their finished book, which means I need a certain number of ideas to help build out those chapters.

Make It So

It is important to find and vet your chosen professional, but it is vital that you take intentional action to move your book forward. Analysis paralysis is a real thing, so make sure you set internal deadlines to make your decision as methodically as possible. When you begin with a clear goal and the end in mind, you will be better able to avoid missteps and wasted time.

CHAPTER 8

Delegate Your Book

It's not time to hire a ghostwriter until you know what your book will be about and who will be reading it. You want to bring your best ideas with you while you are interviewing writers to find the perfect fit. A word of caution here: Don't share the topic of your book beyond generalities with someone you don't yet have a contract with. You need to protect your intellectual property and your energy and make sure that it is a good fit before sharing your fleshed-out idea.

A book coach can step in during the pre-book idea stage to help you plan the flow and create an outline. Sometimes it is easier to write when there is a solid framework in place rather than trying to add words to an empty page. You get the pleasure of writing without the pressure of making it perfect. Your book coach will match your pace and serve as an additional level of accountability to make sure you get your book finished.

How Will You Know When to Pass the Baton?

Delegating your book seems like an easy concept. Come up with a great book idea that furthers your personal and professional goals ... Check. Find the person who can write the way you want readers to experience your book ... Check. You will know it is the right time to pass the baton when the book idea you have can't wait any longer in your head for you to write it.

Start with what comes easy.

Work on the parts of your book that come easy and are of interest to you. If you have a few chapters in mind, it will never hurt to start outlining them. Fill in the pieces that make sense to you now, then reach out for support when you hit a creative block.

Get creative with your available resources.

Delegating your book falls within a wide budget range. You can work with a book coach on an hourly basis to get started and call in a ghostwriter later on in the project if you get stuck. Time can be a scarcer resource than money, and you will want to be realistic about what you have to work with. Have a daily commute? Use the drive time to dictate notes about your next chapter.

Delegate to complement your strengths.

If you are a strong writer and enjoy doing it, commit your thoughts to paper and get through as many chapters as you can. A book coach can guide your writing to the next level by helping you get through creative blocks and polishing each chapter. For the less confident writers, a ghostwriter can help you adapt your ideas into the best words to communicate your vision.

How Long Will It Take?

Writing a book takes a significant amount of time. The great thing about delegating the monumental task is that while the book is in progress, you are still free to pursue your other goals. You will have more time to spend on what matters most to you and won't become discouraged when competing priorities pull at your attention.

Timeline with a book coach

When you work with a book coach, the timeline is most dependent on the pace at which you write. If you can write a chapter a week, you can finish a twelve-chapter book in three to four months. Make sure to allow buffer time in your schedule. A true 1:1 ratio for coaching: chapter is not always possible, especially if you are writing your first book. There may be a challenging chapter or two that needs multiple sessions to iron out.

If you don't have the time to keep up the pace of a chapter a week, the timeline could extend by weeks or months to match the speed at which you are working. Alternately, if you are on fire and churning out chapters a week, you can find a book coach who will meet with you as often as you need.

The key to managing the timeline with a book coach is to book out at least two sessions in advance so you both are on the same page. Many of my book coaching clients enjoy standing appointments—they build their schedule around writing time and find a rhythm early on that works for them.

Timeline with a ghostwriter

The timeline with a ghostwriter is largely dependent on the pace at which the ghostwriter writes and the readiness of information that you have available. The great thing about ghostwriters is that we have a proven process for what we do because we have done it for clients like you many times before. Each time we take on a new client, we are bringing lessons learned and new techniques to make the next project that much better and more efficient.

Each ghostwriter's timeline will vary based on their workload and internal processes, but you can expect something along the lines detailed below:

35,000-word manuscript/120 pages
3 to 6 months
This will be a high-level view of your experience and research. You will have about ten chapters to set the scene and make your recommendations for the industry.

50,000-word manuscript/160 pages
6 to 12 months
This will be an excellent representation of your experience and research. You will have about a dozen chapters to explore the nuances and make your recommendations for the industry.

90,000-word manuscript/270 pages

12 to 18 months

This will be the epitome of your experience and research. You will have more than fifteen chapters to explore the nuances and make your recommendations based on your past success.

The page counts referenced above are based on a standard book size of 6 x 9 inches and include page count for front and back matter.

Remember that your timeline will vary based on your ghostwriter's workflow and the quality and quantity of information you provide. Always ask for an estimated timeline and when the milestones are planned.

CHAPTER 9

Right Words, Right Time

Your book is going to be amazing because it is going to be the best of your ideas and concepts. It will distill your experience and your ideas into a format that your audience needs if they want to move forward with you toward achieving their next goals. It can feel self-serving to write a book and even moreso when you hire someone to write it for you. Take a step back and look at the bigger picture—you are ensuring that the information in your head reaches the people who need it the most.

There is nothing self-serving in sharing what you know so that the people in your community and the wider world can improve their lives and the lives of their loved ones. The words you use—the ones that your book coach draws out of you, or your ghostwriter adapts for you—those words are the right ones to tell your story.

How Will You Know When the Right Words are on the Page?

As a ghostwriter, I know that the right words have landed when the client tells me that they can't remember which parts they wrote and which parts they approved from what I submitted. You will know the right words have been published when your audience tells you that your words resonate, that they have meaning. Long before that, you will know the right words have landed when the ideas you were trying to explain are easily understood by your target market. If you are unsure, take a sample chapter to one of your favorite clients and ask what they think of it.

Look for the words common to your industry and break them down for people outside of your usual network. Start with the words you learned when you were new to your industry, and branch out to the ones covered by continuing education courses.

Focus on the ways your words can make the world a more informed, positive place. The right words will support you and your readers in achieving a common goal. Home in on the way that the words and phrases align with your message, and strike from your vocabulary the words that create in you unease or worry.

List of Influential Words

advisable
adaptable
credible
diligent
enthusiastic
flawless
outstanding
receptive
talented
relevant
strategic
useful

How Will You Know When is the Right Time to Publish?

Releasing your words into the world can be an unsettling time. You may worry about how your words will be perceived and received. The right time for you to publish will be when you have created the best book possible for the topic you want to share. You'll feel this tug to share your message with a larger audience, and there will come a time when you can no longer ignore this call to share your story. That is the time when you should publish.

Everything is permanent, and nothing is permanent. Think about your book's permanence like a permanent marker is permanent. Sure, it is out there for the world to see, but you can always color over it. Also, if you don't do anything to keep the mark fresh, it will fade over time until it is barely visible. Publish a book you will be proud to nurture and keep marketing for years to come.

7 Times to Release a New Book

1. Celebrating a business anniversary
2. Obtaining a new professional certification
3. Announcing a change in services offered
4. Opening a new business
5. Branching out into a new market or territory
6. Preparing to sell your business
7. Reaching a milestone in your success

So What Do You Do Now?

You know the type of book you need to take your business to a higher level, and you know when you want it in your hands. Now your next step is to reverse engineer the process.

Envision the book in your hands. What are you going to do with it? Who is going to read it? What goals will this book help you achieve?

Write down your book idea. What is the main message of your book? What information do you need to make sure to include?

Start interviewing the people who will support you in your book-writing journey. Start at nvisiblewriter.com/bookcoaching or nvisiblewriter.com/ghostwriting for more information on what it is like to work with me. You'll start with Book Coaching if you are pre-idea for your book and Ghostwriting if you want the book done for you.

Make It So

Delegate your book because you have one inside you that needs to come out. You are the only person with your blend of experience and education. Take what you know and share it with the people who need to learn from your process. Do what it takes to get your book done.

The Nonfiction Hero's Journey

The Author as Hero is widely debated. Some critics argue that it is better to have the Client be the Hero portrayed in the story rather than the subject matter expert as the protagonist. Both are outlined below:

Chapter Theme	Author as Hero	Client as Hero
CH 1: Ordinary World	A day in the mundane life of you as the business owner. This is not a time to share a big win or an emotional story; focus on the simple reality of the day-to-day responsibilities of you as the business leader.	A simple, uninspiring day in the life of the client. You can mention adjacent problems they might encounter, but it is too early to bring in major problems that you can fix.

Chapter Theme	Author as Hero	Client as Hero
CH 2: Call to Adventure	Identify the opportunities available to you. This can come in the form of a phone call or message that the reader gets to learn about through your eyes.	Identify the opportunities available to your Hero. Introduce the reader to a new idea through a new character or by using the Hero's inner dialogue.
CH 3: Refusal of the Call	Identify the push and pull of motivations so the reader understands how you are struggling with the decision to accept or reject the call to adventure.	Share the motivations of the Hero with the reader so they understand the struggle to accept or reject the call to adventure.
CH 4: Meeting with the Mentor	Use a moment of internal clarity or reflection to share your growth as a business leader.	As the author, this is an ideal situation to represent your experience and establish yourself as the mentor to the Hero.
CH 5: Crossing the First Threshold	Teach the reader the first step of your process. Describe the first action you take to enact your expertise.	The Hero takes the first step in working with you. Describe the first action you take together.

Chapter Theme	Author as Hero	Client as Hero
CH 6: Tests, Allies, and Enemies	Focus on the training you undergo that builds your expertise. Forces, both internal and external, arise to block your way, but there is still a clear path forward.	The Hero is tested, and the reader is introduced to enemies and allies. The test can be planned or unexpected—be intentional in your choice.
CH 7: Innermost Cave	Emotions are high before the big ordeal. Share what you are feeling with the reader so they understand the tensions at play.	The object of the journey is revealed. The Hero faces great danger before reaching the summit.
CH 8: The Ordeal	This is the low point in your journey. You face the hardest struggle of your career.	The Hero has to fight to make it through this tough situation. They are unsure if they will get through unscathed.
CH 9: Reward	You get closure or relief in what you were working toward. You earn a certification or recognition in your industry.	The Hero achieves their goal. This is a moment of celebration you can share with them.

Chapter Theme	Author as Hero	Client as Hero
CH 10: The Road Back	Your story isn't over. Challenges you face in business continue to surface, but the message is one of optimism.	The Hero is aware of the challenges still to come, though the worst of it is over. They have a renewed energy and resilience.
CH 11: The Resurrection	Your moment of transformation does not come without pain. Share a similarly intense low point as in Chapter 8: The Ordeal.	This is often a replay of the intense emotions in The Ordeal. The Hero faces a transformational experience.
CH 12: Return with the Elixir	This encapsulates the end result of the big breakthrough. Your reader should have a thorough understanding of your expertise and the results you can provide.	The Hero emerges changed for the better from the journey. The reader should feel satisfied and have a desire to start their own journey.

Glossary

avatar A representation of your ideal client or reader.

back matter Publishing industry term referring to information located at the end of the book. This includes material like the appendixes, glossary, endotes, list of contributors, index, and about the author.

book coach The person who guides the author in completing their manuscript. Sessions usually last an hour and can range in style based on the unique skillset of the individual book coach. Consider approaches like mindset training, motivation, and editing to name a few.

bulk book sales Sales of a book ranging from ten copies and above in a single transaction. This is common for events and trainings where an organization is purchasing for departments or groups or an event planner is purchasing for a conference or summit.

copyediting Editing service covering grammatical mistakes, spelling, punctuation, word choice, and issues of consistency in tone or style. The publisher usually includes a copy editor as part of the package, so there is not a need to hire one on your own unless you are self-publishing.

developmental editing Editing service which includes a high-level view, focusing on structure more than punctuation and grammar. If you get stuck midway through writing a manuscript, a developmental editor may be able to dig you out and put you back on the path to finishing the book. This service is not usually covered by a publishing contract.

dialogue Written conversation recorded for the reader. In nonfiction, this dialogue does not need to be verbatim but does need to keep with the spirit of the original conversation.

digital shelf Casual reference to platforms where eBooks can be read such as Apple iBooks, Amazon Kindle, Barnes & Noble Press, Hoopla, et cetera.

eBook A finished book made available in digital form.

editor The person who can help the author clearly communicate ideas and avoid embarrassment from errors large and small.

Everyman A literary device originally sourced from *The Summoning of Everyman*, a late fifteenth-century morality play. The premise is that the ordinary and humble character serves as a stand-in for the audience to identify directly with that character.

fiction Writing that describes imagined events and people.

front matter Publishing industry term that refers to the information traditionally placed at the front of the book including title pages, copyright page, dedication, foreword, acknowledgements and table of contents.

ghostwriter Professional writer who uses the author's ideas to create a finished manuscript.

Hero The protagonist of the story. Based on Joseph Campbell's *The Hero's Journey*, the idea is there are universal themes present that the Hero encounters and overcomes in the course of their story.

hybrid or "indie" publisher A nontraditional publisher, sometimes called an independent publisher is an entity that supports authors in their publishing journey. Unlike a traditional publisher, an independent publisher offers the author more customization and control over the published manuscript.

manuscript This is the name of your book before it becomes an official book with a title.

monologue Historically used in a stage setting, a monologue can be used in nonfiction to give the reader added insight into the narrator's context for a specific scene or situation.

nonfiction Writing that describes real-life events and people.

proofreading Editing service that is the final run-through double-checks for spelling errors, punctuation mishaps, and poor word choice with an added layer of a visual check for consistency with page numbers and headings, as well as bad line breaks. Even if your publisher offers an in-house copyeditor, you may benefit from hiring your own proofreader before signing off on the proof.

publisher A company that serves the author to get their book to market in a professional and high-quality manner.

self-publishing The author sources vendors to edit and format their book. There can be a wide range of quality and a steep learning curve to put out a product that meets industry standard.

Recommended Reading

Big Goals, Lasting Legacy

- *A New Earth: Awakening to Your Life's Purpose* by Eckhart Tolle
- *Designing Your Life: How to Build a Well-Lived, Joyful Life* by Bill Burnett and Dave Evans
- *We: A Manifesto for Women Everywhere* by Gillian Anderson and Jennifer Nadel

Find Your Story

- *The Hero with a Thousand Faces* by Joseph Campbell
- *The Writer's Journey: Mythic Structure for Writers* by Christopher Vogler
- *Rising Strong* by Brené Brown

Attract Your Audience

- *Bad Bitches and Power Pitches* by Precious Williams

- *The Storytelling Edge* by Shane Snow and Joe Lazauskas
- *Youtility: Why Smart Marketing is About Help Not Hype* by Jay Baer

Enjoy Your Voice

- *Say It Well: Creating and Tailoring Value-Driven Communication* by Derek Lott
- *Speak*: *Find Your Voice, Trust Your Gut, and Get From Where You Are to Where You Want to Be* by Tunde Oyeneyin
- *The Creative Habit: Learn It and Use It for Life* by Twyla Tharp

About the Author

Chrissy Das is a nonfiction ghostwriter, book coach, and editor who founded (i)nvisible writer to serve service-based business owners and creative professionals who want to use the best words to communicate life-changing ideas. They rely on Chrissy to help them better communicate their thought leadership and grow their businesses.

Since 2015, Chrissy has ghostwritten more than a dozen books with authors across such industries as accounting, legal, nonprofit, real estate, and psychology. "She has a unique way of drawing you into her world with her skills of writing and storytelling," one client explains. "Chrissy is a giving collaborator, focused on making her projects perfect for everyone involved."

She earned a bachelor's degree in English literature with a minor in women's studies from Georgia College & State University and credits her year studying abroad in the United Kingdom with her unique sense of place and humor. Chrissy loves to recount studying English Literature in the U.S. and American Literature in the

U.K. and encourages her clients to read cross-continent and cross-industry to tap into creative veins.

Chrissy lives in Jacksonville, Florida, with her husband and their dog, Neil.

GHOSTWRITING ——————

Learn more
about working
with Chrissy
@
nvisiblewriter.com

——————BOOK COACHING

CPSIA information can be obtained
at www.ICGtesting.com
Printed in the USA
JSHW040752131222
34801JS00006B/21

9 781953 315243